SHOCK ZONE™
TRUE SURVIVAL STORIES

SuRVIVING
NATURAL
DISASTERS

BY MARCIA AMIDON LUSTED

Lerner Publications Company • Minneapolis

Cover image: A Family navigates a
flooded street in Thailand in 2011.

Lerner Publications Company
A division of Lerner Publishing Group, Inc.
241 First Avenue North
Minneapolis, MN 55401 U.S.A.

For updated reading levels and more information, look up this title
at www.lernerbooks.com

Library of Congress Cataloging-in-Publication Data

Lusted, Marcia Amidon.
    Surviving natural disasters / by Marcia Amidon Lusted.
        pages   cm. — (Shockzone—true survival stories)
    Includes index.
    ISBN 978–1–4677–1438–9 (lib. bdg. : alk. paper)
    ISBN 978–1–4677–2519–4 (eBook)
    1. Survival. 2. Natural disasters. I. Title.
    G525.L87 2014
    363.34—dc23   2013021104

Manufactured in the United States of America
1–PC–12/31/13

TABLE OF CONTENTS

WHEN DISASTER STRIKES

What is the worst natural disaster you've ever survived? Has a blizzard knocked out your power? Has a flood closed roads near your house? Maybe you've even been through a hurricane or a tornado. Some of the **scariest survival stories** come from natural disasters such as these. But some disasters do more than just cause a few days without electricity or a snow day from school. Some disasters sweep away homes, crush buildings and cars, and kill and injure people.

Natural disasters put people in dangerous, life-threatening situations every day. Against all odds, some people survive these terrifying events and live to tell their stories. Read on for real-life stories of deadly and devastating natural disasters. If a natural disaster strikes where you live, you might end up with a similar survival story of your own.

Some natural disasters can wipe out entire neighborhoods in minutes.

Trapped Under the Rubble

On January 12, 2010, a massive earthquake struck the island nation of Haiti in the Caribbean Sea. The ground rippled and shifted. Buildings made of cement blocks crumbled and collapsed. In just twenty seconds, little was left in some areas but rubble and dirt. In the capital city of Port-au-Prince, eight-year-old Kiki Joachin was buried in the rubble of his six-story apartment building. His mother had been making dinner when the quake began. "The whole building fell flat in seconds," she later said. Kiki was trapped alongside his eleven-year-old sister Sabrina and his four-year-old brother Titite. The bodies of two other sisters were nearby. They died instantly when the building fell.

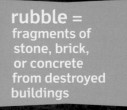

rubble = fragments of stone, brick, or concrete from destroyed buildings

Kiki was trapped for eight days. "When our house fell down, I thought I was going to die," he said. On the fifth day, he saw his younger brother die in front of him. He remembers crying as Sabrina covered Titite with her T-shirt.

Firefighters from around the world worked tirelessly to rescue victims of the earthquake.

After eight days, Kiki and Sabrina were giving up hope. But then a neighbor who was searching the ruins heard Kiki's faint cry. "Mama! Help us, Mama! Water!" The neighbor found two firefighters from the United States. They had come to Haiti to help after the earthquake. Chris Dunic and Brad Antons spent four hours carefully drilling through the rubble.

They finally reached Kiki and his sister. At first Kiki was afraid of them, because they wore helmets and face masks and carried a jackhammer. "The hardest thing was getting the kid to come up," Dunic said. "We were scaring him." Finally, Kiki's neighbor convinced him to come up. As Dunic reached in and pulled him up, Kiki's face broke into a huge grin. "I smiled because I was free," he told reporters. "I smiled because I was alive."

THE RICHTER SCALE

The 2010 Haiti earthquake measured 7.0 on the Richter scale. The Richter scale is a tool that scientists use to measure the strength of an earthquake. It measures the total energy released by a quake. Each number is ten times stronger than the previous one. So a 7.0 quake is ten times more powerful than a 6.0 quake. Any quake over 6 is considered to be severe.

Kiki (*in green*) and his sister Sabrina (*in pink*) survived for an amazing eight days in the rubble of their home.

No one knew that Shinkawa was 10 miles (16 km) out at sea. He had been on the second floor of his home when a wave crashed through the windows. Suddenly, everything went black. "I was terrified. I couldn't see anything. I tried to swim," he remembered. His head finally broke through the surface of the water, and he searched desperately for anything to cling to. "I swam towards the roof," Shinkawa recalled. "I didn't feel the cold, but I just needed something to hang on to. It took me four attempts to haul myself up onto the roof."

Huge areas of Japan were left underwater by the rushing waters of the tsunami.

Moments later, the roof was swept off the house and out into the Pacific Ocean. "I was washed out to sea and in the night all I could hear was the grinding of the debris in the water around me," he said. The next day, Shinkawa waved at six different helicopters that passed near him. But they didn't see him. At night, Shinkawa wrapped himself in a soggy blanket and tried to stay warm. The skin on his hands and face was turning white from the salt water. "I thought about my family that night and how I wanted to be at home with them again," he said.

debris = pieces of destroyed objects or structures

Two days after drifting out to sea, Shinkawa noticed a nearby ship. He knew it might be his last hope for survival. Thinking quickly, he made a flag using a piece of red cloth and a stick. He waved the flag. "The ship slowly turned towards me and they started flashing a light in my direction, so I knew that they had seen me at last," he said. He was finally rescued. "The taste of that first drink they gave me aboard the ship was wonderful."

Shinkawa (*right*) survived for forty-three hours on his rooftop.

BURIED ALIVE IN AN ICY TOMB

"I saw lights. . . . I shouted a lot." That's how skier Cedric Genoud described being buried in snow in February of 2010. The searchlights of nighttime rescuers passed over him. But they did not hear him shouting. Genoud had set off to ski by himself on a mountain near the Swiss village of Evolene. But instead of staying on public trails, he decided to ski in an area that was marked as an avalanche risk. "I started on a north facing slope, the snow was holding well," he said. "Then I moved to a sunny spot."

The snow gave way suddenly. It dragged him down the slopew. Genoud quickly realized an avalanche was starting. He thought it would be a small one. He expected he would easily be able to avoid it. But before he knew it, he was buried under 3 feet (1 m) of snow. He could not move his arms or legs— just his head. Using his helmet, he created a tiny space to breathe. But he was still trapped in an icy tomb.

"It was like a sarcophagus, like having concrete around me," Genoud said. "I kept on telling myself that I mustn't give up, that people loved me." The next morning, Genoud got lucky. A rescue helicopter spotted the top of his helmet. "It was one of the most marvelous moments of my life," he said. Most people who are trapped under tons of snow only survive for a few minutes because they can't breathe. Thanks to his breathing space, Genoud survived for seventeen hours.

sarcophagus
= a stone coffin

HYPOTHERMIA
Most people who are trapped by avalanches die from lack of air, shock, or hypothermia. Hypothermia occurs when the body has such a low temperature that its normal functions stop. At first the person shivers and is confused. Then movements become slow and clumsy. Lips, ears, fingers, and toes may turn blue. Eventually the heart and the brain stop working, causing the person to die.

A Fiery Volcano

On May 18, 1980, Sue Ruff and Bruce Nelson, both twenty-two, were camping with friends. The group was 14 miles (23 km) from Mount St. Helens in Washington State. They were toasting marshmallows over the fire for breakfast. Suddenly the volcanic mountain erupted. "We saw this thick yellow-and-black cloud rushing towards us," Ruff said. "I remember thinking, 'I should take a picture of it.' Then I thought we'd better hide."

As trees were uprooted all around them from the force of the volcanic blast, Ruff and Nelson were blown into a deep hole left by an uprooted tree. More trees and thick ash fell all around them. They were buried and could barely breathe. "Sue and I started digging our way out of the ash," Nelson said. "Our mouths were full of mud. I told Sue we were going to die and she said 'Nonsense.'"

As they clawed their way out of the ash, hot stones raining from the sky hit them on the head. Chunks of ice as big as cars were blown from the top of the peak and crashed down around them. They gagged from the ash and choked on the gas fumes from the volcano. Ruff and Nelson covered their noses and mouths with their sweatshirts after digging their way out of the hole.

They found two friends, Brian Thomas and Dan Balch. Balch had been badly burned. The heat blast of the explosion had melted the skin off his arms. Thomas had a broken hip from being struck by a falling tree. Ruff and Nelson helped their friends. Then they started wading through knee-deep ash to get help. Helicopters eventually rescued the campers. "When we were up there, we didn't know if we'd get out of there alive," Nelson later said. "We had several hours to think, 'We still could die.'"

The eruption of Mount St. Helens blew the top off the mountain and left deep layers of ash and debris for miles around.

Trapped by Katrina

Search crews spread through New Orleans, Louisiana, looking for survivors. It was August 2005. It had been eighteen days since the rushing floodwaters caused by Hurricane Katrina devastated the city. As Katrina neared the coastline, its gusts had measured more than 170 miles (273 km) per hour. As much as 1 inch (2.5 centimeters) of rain had fallen per hour in its path. It was one of the strongest storms to hit the southeastern United States in the past one hundred years. And New Orleans was directly in its path.

devastated = destroyed or ruined

One crew's search-and-rescue boat moved along Painters Street and checked each house. All they found were dead bodies. They did not expect to hear a voice shout, "Hey, over here!" It was coming from a one-story wooden house.

Two crew members used a sledgehammer to break through the water-swollen front door. They struggled to move through the living room filled with soggy, overturned furniture. Finally, they entered the grimy kitchen and found Gerald Martin, aged seventy-six, sitting in a chair. Martin had been trapped in his home for eighteen days without food or contact with other people. He was very relieved to see the rescue team. And he was very thirsty. The team gave a huge joyous shout at finding someone still alive in the house. How had Martin survived?

After Hurricane Katrina, rescuers in boats searched for survivors.

Thousands of New Orleans residents went through situations similar to the one faced by Gerald Martin.

Martin told rescuers, "I was living in the attic for 16 days, and I was living off water." Martin's family had left the area before Katrina hit, but he stayed to go to church. Then he took a nap. When he woke up, his house was filling with water. He had just enough time to grab some drinking water and climb into his attic. Martin described the attic as feeling like an oven after days of extreme heat. It would have been even worse but a fallen tree provided a little bit of shade. He sipped at his small supply of water, but it ran out several days before he was rescued.

Finally, Martin was able to move down to his kitchen after sixteen days in the attic when floodwaters receded from the bottom floor of the house. But the water outside kept him from leaving his home. The power was still out, and he couldn't call for help.

Martin was the first trapped person to be found alive in his neighborhood. When he emerged from his house, he had to hold his pants up because he had lost so much weight. The rescuers were overjoyed to have finally found a survivor. "We've been in rescue mode the whole time and haven't given up hope that there was someone out there alive," said one of the crew members.

As Martin was helped into a waiting helicopter to be taken to a hospital, he asked if they could stop at a fast food restaurant to get a taco. "He was weak, very tired, but he was able to speak, able to stand," said a rescuer. "He was very relieved. He was very thirsty. He was in good spirits."

SAFFIR-SIMPSON SCALE

The Saffir-Simpson Hurricane Wind Scale is a scale of 1 to 5 that rates a hurricane's strength by its wind speed. Hurricane Katrina had a Saffir-Simpson rating of 3. This is strong enough to cause severe damage in the affected area.

Category	Winds in mph (kmh)	Damage
1	74–95 (119–153)	Minimal
2	96–110 (154–177)	Moderate
3	111–129 (178–208)	Extensive
4	130–156 (209–251)	Extreme
5	More than 157 (252)	Catastrophic

Gerald Martin was the first survivor found by the rescue team in its twelve days of searching.

A STRANGE LIGHT IN THE SKY

On a sleepy afternoon in November 1954, Ann Elizabeth Hodges wasn't feeling very well. The Sylacauga, Alabama, resident decided to take a nap on her living room sofa. She was awakened by a crash as an object fell through the ceiling. It bounced off a radio, then hit her on her left hip. Was it something from upstairs, falling through the ceiling? Nope. The object was out of this world. Ann Hodges had just become the only known case of a person being struck by a meteorite. Crashing through the house had slowed the space rock. But the 8-pound (4-kilogram) meteorite still left a bruise the size of a grapefruit on her hip.

meteorite = a lump of stone or metal that falls to the Earth from outer space

The rock had attracted attention as a bright light streaking through the sky. It made loud booming noises as it broke the sound barrier. Crowds of people showed up at the Hodges's home when they learned the meteorite had actually hit her. The US Air Force also arrived to investigate. The nosy people frustrated Ann's husband, Eugene. He became angry when police took the meteorite away without permission. He had hoped to make some money from selling the space rock. But after legal battles, that never happened

"I feel like the meteorite is mine," Ann later said. "After all, it hit me!"

The rock was eventually returned to the Hodgeses, but by that time no one wanted to purchase it. They ended up using the meteorite as a doorstop until Ann gave it to the Alabama Museum of Natural History in March 1956. It can still be seen there today. Ann later had a nervous breakdown and died at the age of fifty-two in 1972. Her husband blamed the media frenzy for her death. He claimed Ann never recovered from the stress surrounding the meteorite.

METEORS, METEOROIDS, AND METEORITES

What's the difference between a meteor, a meteoroid, and a meteorite? It's simple—the different names just describe the same object at different times. When a rock is floating through space, it is a meteoroid. When it enters Earth's atmosphere, it begins to heat up and glow as it smashes into air molecules. This shining, streaking rock is called a meteor. Finally, after it hits the ground, it is known as a meteorite.

The meteorite left a hole in Ann Hodges's ceiling and damaged her radio.

Riding the Floodwaters

"I don't think we're going to make it," Roger Oldham told his wife, Bonnie. They were trapped on the roof of their house, which was being swept through their hometown by raging floodwaters. Rain battered down on them, and the wind howled. No one could hear their cries for help. It was August 2007 in Stockton, Minnesota.

Roger, his wife, and his mother-in-law had fled to the roof when floodwaters began surrounding their one-story house. He had seen water rushing down a drainage ditch next to the house. He knew they had to get to high ground as soon as possible. The roof was the nearest and best option. Bonnie grabbed a few blankets for protection. Meanwhile, Roger stacked a glass patio table and a wooden desk so they could climb up to the roof. Moments after they scrambled onto the roof, floodwaters blew out the house's foundation. It sounded like a tremendous explosion. They felt the house moving under them.

A neighbor looked outside and was shocked to see the family floating through town. "They were on the roof screaming and there was nothing you could do," the neighbor said. The house drifted for about 1,000 feet (300 m) before it slammed into railroad tracks. The tracks kept it from moving any farther. Though the house had stopped, the Oldhams were still trapped. They spent a long night screaming for help. Firefighters finally spotted them early the next morning. Their only injuries were cuts and scratches.

When the Oldham family returned to see where their house had stood, they found only a hole filled with dirty water. "Everything's gone," Bonnie remembered thinking when she saw the hole. "I ain't gonna build here again," Roger later said to a reporter. "I think I'll move out of town."

If not for the railroad tracks that stopped their house, the Oldhams may not have survived the powerful flooding.

Carried by a Tornado

"Ever been in a deep sleep and someone's yelling, but you can barely hear them? It was something like that. I could hear everything, feel stuff, but I couldn't see anything." That's how Rick Boland described being lifted and carried about 100 yards (90 m) by a tornado. It was August 2006 in Saint Mary, Missouri. Late in the evening, his son Craig said, "The sky's looking funny out here." Moments later, the lights flickered and the wind began to howl. The house shook back and forth. Small objects were blown off the deck.

Rick, Craig, and Craig's girlfriend ran to a bathroom on the top floor of the house. Boland told them to get into the bathtub. When he looked at the floor under his feet, it seemed to be rippling like waves in water. He was having trouble keeping his balance. Just then, the power went out, leaving the small group in pitch-black darkness. "I heard windows blowing out, stuff smacking," said Boland. "It was like a big tidal wave hit the house. It was the loudest thing I ever heard in my life."

Tornadoes are capable of ripping apart a house in moments.

Suddenly it felt like a giant hand picked up the house. Boland remembered hearing a humming sound, like a giant vacuum cleaner. It was then that the house fell apart. Boland realized he was being carried into the sky by the tornado. "I had my eyes closed, just keeping the wind and debris from getting in," Boland said. "I was being struck by debris but couldn't really feel it. I just felt a deep pain." He spun around violently in the air. Then he crashed to the ground on his stomach. He glanced up, and lightning struck nearby. The bolt lit up the entire tornado for a split second. "It was the first tornado I'd ever seen," Boland remembered.

Boland, Craig, and Craig's girlfriend all landed in a neighbor's field. They were about 20 yards (18 m) from one another. Miraculously, all three had survived being carried by the tornado. But just barely. Boland had about thirty pieces of wood sticking into his body, ranging in size from a few inches to several feet long. He figured they were probably all pieces of the destroyed bathroom walls and floor. The three of them lay in the field waiting for an ambulance when they heard the tornado warning sirens going off. Boland remembered thinking, "Well, they're a little late."

Emergency medical responders can become overwhelmed by the massive destruction caused by tornadoes.

10 Supplies for Natural Disasters

You never know when a natural disaster can strike. Here are ten things to have on hand, just in case:

1. Water: Keep a supply of 1 gallon (3.8 liters) per person, per day, for at least three days.

2. Food: Have at least a three-day supply of food for each person.

3. Radio: Use a radio to receive weather alerts or news updates. Make sure to have a battery-powered or hand-crank radio in case the electricity goes out.

4. Flashlight: Use a flashlight to see in the dark and signal for rescuers. Have an extra set of batteries as backup.

5. First aid kit: Use soap to clean wounds, bandages to help patch up minor cuts or other injuries, and aspirin to reduce pain.

6. Dust masks, plastic sheeting, and duct tape: Protect against dust or poison released by the disaster using plastic sheeting and dust masks.

7. Wrench or pliers: Use tools to turn off appliances, such as gas ovens. This can prevent explosions.

8. Manual can opener: Have a can opener to open food containers.

9. Local maps: Disasters such as tornadoes or hurricanes can make your own neighborhood unrecognizable. Have a map in case you need to find your way around.

10. A cell phone with a solar charger: Use a cell phone to call for help or contact friends and family.

Fleischer, Paul. *Weatherwise: Lightning, Hurricanes, and Blizzards; The Science of Storms.* Minneapolis: Lerner Publications Company, 2010.
Check out this book to learn about how severe storms form and why they are so destructive.

Higgins, Nadia. *Natural Disasters through Infographics.* Minneapolis: Lerner Publications Company, 2013.
This book uses cool infographics to show Earth's climate and weather systems and why some natural disasters occur.

O'Sullivan, Joanne. *Bizarre Weather: Howling Winds, Pouring Rain, Blazing Heat, Freezing Cold, Hurricanes, Earthquakes, Tsunamis, Tornadoes, and More of Nature's Fury.* Somerville, MA: Charlesbridge Publishing, 2013.
Learn about some of the strangest types of severe storms that have occurred, such as worm showers and watermelon rain!

Reilly, Kathleen M. *Natural Disasters: Investigate Earth's Most Destructive Forces with 25 Projects.* White River Junction, VT: Nomad Press, 2012.
This site is a great way to explore natural disasters with many cool hands-on projects to build.

Royston, Angela. *Science Fights Back: Science vs. Natural Disasters.* New York: Gareth Stevens, 2013.
Learn about the different ways that science is attempting to prevent or combat natural disasters and some of the issues surrounding their efforts.

Watts, Clare, and Trevor Day. *Natural Disasters.* **DK Eyewitness Books series.** New York: DK Publishing, 2012.
Explore many different types of natural disasters and the damage they cause, with plenty of amazing photographs on every page.

LERNER

Expand learning beyond the printed book. Download free, complementary educational resources for this book from our website, www.lerneresource.com.

SOURCE

6   Lukas I. Alpert, "Miracle Boy: 'I Smiled Because I Was Alive,'" *New York Post*, January 22, 2010, http://www.nypost.com/p/news/international/miracle_boy_smiled_because_was_alive_wgOJ8u4X5k7wU23uF6RAOL.

6   Kenneth Miller, "Miracle Boy Survivor of the Haiti Earthquake," *Reader's Digest*, February 2011, http://www.rd.com/true-stories/survival/miracleboy-survivor-of-the-haiti-earthquake.

7   Alpert, "Miracle Boy: 'I Smiled Because I Was Alive.'"

7   Miller, "Miracle Boy Survivor of the Haiti Earthquake."

10 Julian Ryall, "Japan Earthquake and Tsunami: The Man Who Floated Out to Sea on His House Remembers the Tragedy," *Telegraph* (London), March 2, 2012, http://www.telegraph.co.uk/news/worldnews/asia/japan/9116267/Japan-earthquake-and-tsunami-the-man-who-floated-out-to-sea-on-hishouse-remembers-the-tragedy.html.

11 Ibid.

12 Adam Arnold, "'Miracle' Skier Survives 17 Hours under Snow," *Sky News*, February 9, 2010, http://news.sky.com/story/758011/miracle-skiersurvives-17-hours-under-snow.

13 Ibid.

14 "God I Want to Live!" *Time*, June 2, 1980, http://www.time.com/time/magazine/article/0,9171,924152,00.html.

15 "Couple Who Fled Eruption Discover Life Has Changed," *Spokane Daily Chronicle*, January 16, 1981, 22, http://news.google.com/newspapers?nid=1338&dat=19810116&id=SqYSAAAAIBAJ&sjid=SPkDAAAAIBAJ&pg=5126,115913.

16 "76-Year-Old Man Found after 18 Days," *NBC News*, September 19, 2005, http://www.nbcnews.com/id/9376860/ns/us_news-katrina_the_long_road_back/t/-year-old-man-found-after-days.

18 Ibid.

19 Ibid.

21 Justin Nobel, "The True Story of History's Only Known Meteorite Victim," *National Geographic*, February 20, 2013, http://news.nationalgeographic.com/news/2013/02/130220-russia-meteorite-annhodges-science-space-hit.

22 "Flood Survivor: 'I Don't Think We're Going to Make It,'" *MPR News*, August 19, 2007, http://minnesota.publicradio.org/display/web/2007/08/19/survivor.

13 Ibid.

24 Rick Boland, "What It Feels Like...to be Carried by a Tornado," *Esquire*, April 28, 2011, http://www.esquire.com/features/what-it-feelslike/ESQ0806WIFL_114_5.

25 Ibid.

26 Ibid.

27 Ibid.

PHOTO ACKNOWLEDGMENTS

The images in this book are used with the permission of: © Martin Haas/Shutterstock Images, pp. 4, 25; © Jocelyn Augustino/FEMA, p. 5; © arindambanerjee/Shutterstock Images, p. 6; © Francois Mori/AP Images, p. 7 (top); © Bernard Wis/Paris Match/Getty Images, p. 7 (bottom); © Kyodo News/AP Images, p. 8; Lance Cpl. Ethan Johnson/US Marine Corps, p. 9; © Stocktrek Images/Thinkstock, p. 10; © Defense Ministry/AP Images, p. 11; © My Good Images/Shutterstock Images, p. 12; © AP Images, p. 13; Harry Glicken/USGS, p. 14; Tom Casadevall/USGS, p. 15; NASA, p. 16; © Eric Gay/AP Images, p. 17; © David J. Phillip/AP Images, p. 18; © Rex Ianson/FEMA/AP Images, p. 19; © Krasowit/Shutterstock Images, p. 20; © Bettmann/Corbis/AP Images, p. 21; © Brian Peterson/The Star Tribune/AP Images, p. 22; © Melissa Carlo/The Daily News/AP Images, p. 23; © Todd Shoemake/Shutterstock Images, p. 24; © Ted S. Warren/Austin American-Statesman/AP Images, p. 26; © Orlin Wagner/AP Images, p. 27; © Dave Martin/AP Images, p. 28; © Iwona Grodzka/Shutterstock Images, p. 29.
Front Cover: © iStockphoto.com/gdagys